Zoey the Rainbow Dump truck

by J. W. HUTCHINSON

BIRDVIEW BOOKS

Birdview Books
30650 Rancho California Rd
Suite D40
Temecula, CA 92591

www.JWHutchinson.com
Print ISBN: 979-8-9882160-0-1
The illustrations in this book
were created using pen, ink and watercolor.

On the outside, Zoey the dump truck
seemed pretty ordinary.
But in her heart she knew she could FLY!
And that made her quite extraordinary!

Each day the feeling inside her grew.
She wanted to dump out rainbows not dirt!
She had to tell the crew!

She told her friends about her big, colorful dreams.
But sometimes that's not as easy as it seems.

"I have a dream," said Zoey "that I can FLY!"
"I'm dumping out *rainbows* when I'm up in the sky!"

"That's ridiculous." said Bizzy.
"Now c'mon Zoey, get real!"

"We need more DIRT around here *not* rainbows!"
"Now take the day off and see how you feel."

Zoe felt confused after talking to Bizzy
so she went over to see her friend Diz E.

"I bet ya didn't know I could FLY!"
Zoey teased as Diz E poured the concrete.
"And I'm gonna dump out *rainbows* instead of dirt!"
"Won't that be neat?!"
Diz E was startled by what he heard!

He laughed at Zoey and said "That's absurd! Everyone knows a truck can't fly like a bird!"

Diz E's words made her cry
but she gave it another try!
She drove up to Zak the bulldozer
and told HIM she can fly!

Zoey drove back down the hill
feeling discouraged and quite flustered.

Then she saw her friend Dinky.
He always had a smile!

His job was planting trees!

They stopped and talked
for a while.

"Don't listen to the others," said Dinky.
"Listen to your HEART!" "If dumping out rainbows
is what you truly love to do, then RIGHT NOW
is when you start!"

"I believe in you Zoey!" said Dinky.
"We can use more rainbows around here!"

"Now get up there and get flyin'!"
"And bring us some good cheer!"

It Was easy as can be!

2 3 4!

Her wheels left the floor!

Flying way up high!
Dumping rainbows in the sky!